ISBN 1 85854 362 2
© Brimax Books Ltd 1996. All rights reserved.
Published by Brimax Books Ltd, Newmarket, England CB8 7AU 1996.
Printed in China.

MY READY TO READ STORIES

by
Lucy Kincaid

Illustrated by
Gill Guile

Brimax · Newmarket · England

Contents

A New Friend   8

A Bucket for Dizzy   16

Visitors   28

The Birthday Party   38

New Shoes for Harriet   48

Mud   60

Atishoo!   70

Waves   86

A New Friend

Bert the bear lives in a caravan. His horse, Harriet, pulls the caravan for him. Every day they travel through the countryside. Every evening, Bert finds a field where Harriet can rest and eat her dinner. At night they sleep under the stars.

One evening, as Bert fetches Harriet's bucket from under the caravan, he hears a noise. It is coming from Harriet's bucket. Bert can hear a croaky voice saying, "Go away! Croak! Croak! Leave me alone..." Whatever can it be?

Harriet hears the voice, too. Then she sees a little frog sitting in her bucket!

"Tip it out!" shouts Harriet.

"I'll take it back to the stream," says Bert.

"Oh, please don't do that," says the frog. "Please take me with you. I won't be any trouble! Croak! Croak!"

"You can't live in my bucket," says Harriet.

"Then we'll buy another one," says Bert.

"Oh! All right!" says Harriet.

The little frog jumps onto the grass and starts spinning round with excitement.

"My name is Dizzy," he says.

Harriet shakes her head. "I have always thought frogs were silly," she says.

A Bucket for Dizzy

The next morning, Bert and Harriet set off with Dizzy sitting in Harriet's bucket. It is very hot. Bert makes a paper hat for Harriet to keep the sun off her head.
"Does it look silly?" asks Harriet.
"Yes," says Dizzy. But Harriet does not mind. She is very hot.

Harriet stops to have a drink from her bucket. Dizzy climbs out.

"You won't drink all the water, will you?" he asks.

"This water is for drinking, not for sitting in!" says Harriet.

"But I'll shrivel up without water," says Dizzy. Suddenly Bert takes a cupful of water from the bucket.

"Hop in there, Dizzy," he says. "Then Harriet has enough water to drink, and you have enough to water to keep wet."

Harriet drinks the rest of her water. Dizzy sits in the cup, next to Bert. There isn't much water to keep Dizzy wet. It grows hotter and hotter. Harriet's feet begin to drag. "We'll have to find water soon," says Bert.

Suddenly, Dizzy sniffs the air. "Bring the bucket and follow me," he shouts to Bert. "I'll find some water for you." He jumps out of the cup and onto the road. Bert tries to follow Dizzy. Dizzy hops faster and faster. At last he sees a little stream and dives in.

When Bert catches up with Dizzy, he is floating down the stream. As Bert fills the bucket with water, he hears a shout. It is Dizzy.

"Look what I have found," he says. Bert goes to look and sees an old, dented bucket.

"May I have this bucket as my home?" asks Dizzy.

"Only if it holds water," says Bert. They both watch for leaks as Bert fills the bucket. There are none.

Bert walks back to the caravan carrying two buckets.

"What have you got there?" asks Harriet. "And where is that frog?"

"I'm here," says Dizzy, popping his head out of his very own bucket. "This is my bucket," he says.

"That's a relief," says Harriet, and she drinks all her water. When Bert goes back to the stream to fill her bucket again, Harriet says to Dizzy, "You're not so bad for a frog, I suppose!"

Visitors

Harriet is not happy. She can see for miles ahead. She does not like to see how far she has to go. Then Harriet sees the cave. She does not like caves. But as soon as Bert sees the cave, he pulls on Harriet's reins. She stops.

"Let's go and explore," he says, taking Dizzy from his bucket.

"Come on, Harriet," says Dizzy. Harriet shakes her head. "I am not going into a cave," she says.

Bert carries Dizzy and the lantern into the cave. It is very dark.
Dizzy makes funny shapes with his own shadow.
Suddenly he hears Harriet calling. Bert and Dizzy hurry outside. They see Harriet staring up at the sky.
"It's a...a..." is all she can say.
"Quickly! Into the cave," says Bert. He pulls Harriet inside, too. She is so frightened, that she closes her eyes as tightly as she can.

"What is it?" asks Dizzy.
"I think it's a flying saucer!" says Bert. Harriet's eyes are still tightly shut.
"What are we going to do?" asks Dizzy. He looks out of the cave.
"We must stay hidden and watch," says Bert.

Suddenly, Bert, Dizzy and Harriet hear a strange noise. The flying saucer lands on the hill. Dizzy jumps into Bert's pocket. Harriet opens her eyes to look. She sees lots of little, green figures jumping from the flying saucer. She closes her eyes tightly again.

"What are they doing?" asks Dizzy.

"They are having a picnic!" says Bert, smiling.
"You'll be telling me they're picking daisies next!" says Harriet.
"They are!" says Bert.
"How dare they!" shouts Harriet. The little, green figures are frightened by the noise. They run back to their flying saucer which takes off into the sky. Harriet shakes her head. "What a strange dream I've just had!" she says. "I dreamt I saw a flying saucer!"

The Birthday Party

That night, Bert, Harriet and Dizzy stop to rest by a stream. Bert tips Dizzy out of his bucket and into the stream. Then he gives Harriet her dinner. Bert looks for the lantern but he cannot find it. He has left it in the cave.

"I put it on the ground when I pulled Harriet into the cave, and I forgot to pick it up," he says.

39

"I suppose I"ll have to stand in the dark," says Harriet.

"You always do stand in the dark," says Dizzy. He sits beside Bert on the caravan steps. Suddenly, Bert hears Harriet calling him. He goes to see if she is all right.

"There is something moving in the water," says Harriet.

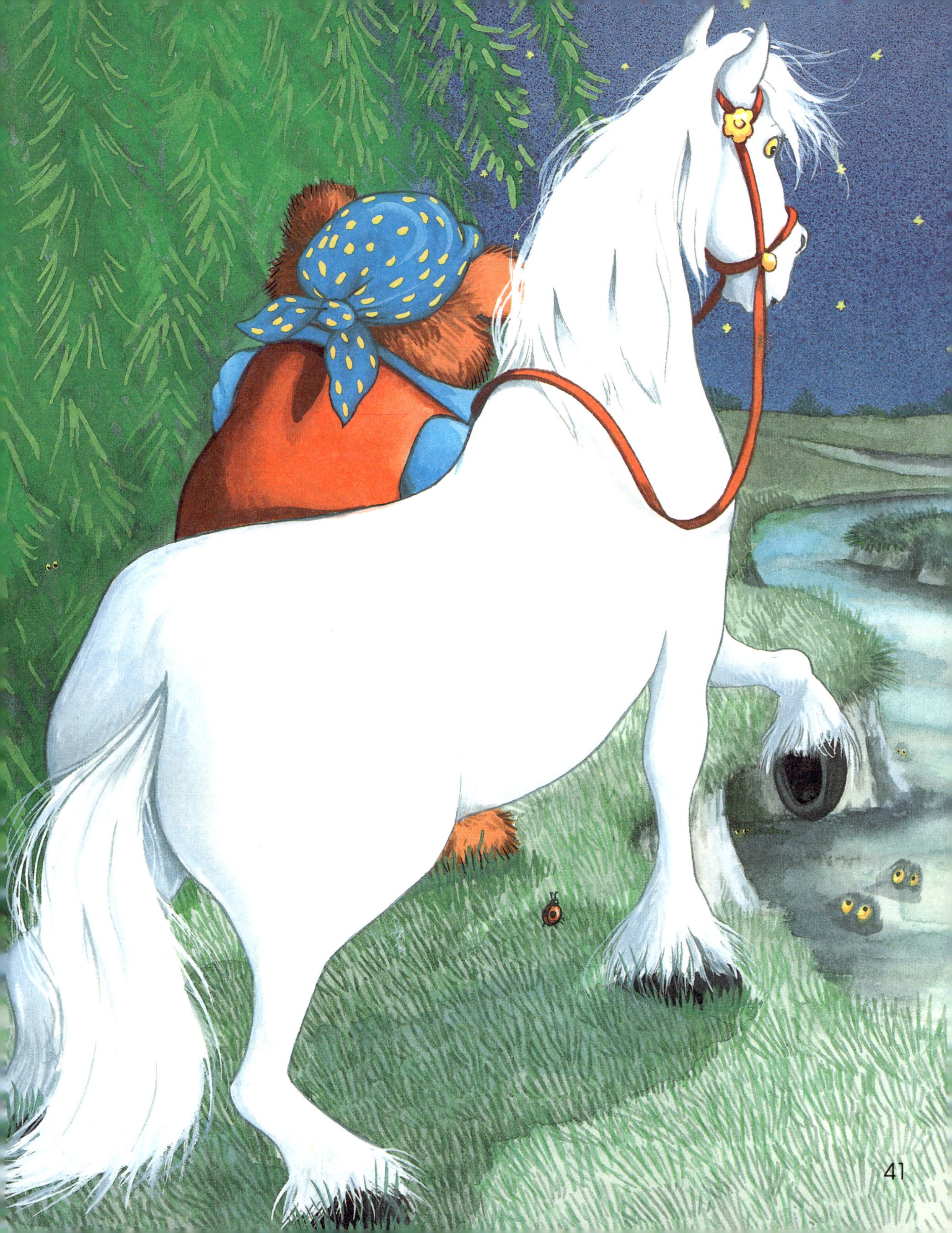

Bert's eyes are getting used to the dark. He sees something move across the grass.
"What is it?" he asks Dizzy.
Dizzy begins to bounce up and down with excitement. "It's frogs! Lots and lots of frogs!"
"Well, go and see what they want," says Harriet. Dizzy jumps away. Then Harriet and Bert hear lots of loud croaking!
"Bert! Save Dizzy!" shouts Harriet. She shuts her eyes tightly.

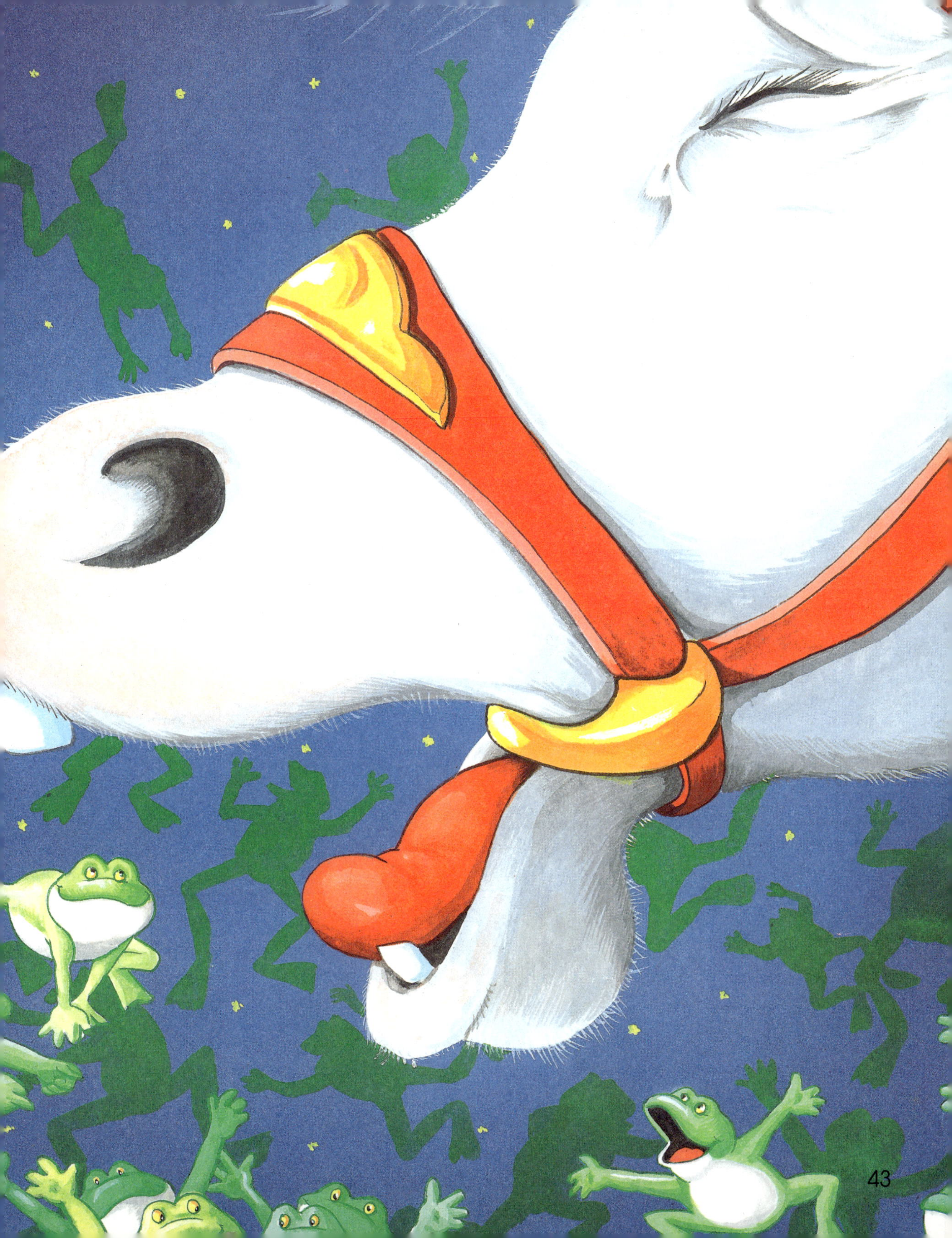

"I don't need saving!" shouts Dizzy, jumping back to his friends. "This is a birthday party. Grandpa Bullfrog is one hundred bullfrog years old today. We are all invited."

Bert decides that he and Harriet should only watch the party. They might tread on someone if they join in. So they watch as the frogs dance and sing songs.

45

It is such a good party that Harriet forgets to sulk about the lantern. She even sings a few songs with her new friends. Early in the morning, the frogs begin their journey home.

"That was the best birthday party I've ever been to," says Dizzy.

"We will go back and fetch the lantern tomorrow," says Bert.

"Let's get some sleep before the sun comes up and the birds start to sing!"

47

New Shoes for Harriet

Harriet's feet are hurting her. She needs some new shoes.
"Horses don't wear shoes!" says Dizzy. When Bert shows him the metal shoes nailed to Harriet's feet, Dizzy is very surprised. Harriet is so grumpy, that Bert decides to take her to the blacksmith. They leave the caravan behind.

49

Dizzy sits on Bert's shoulder as he walks along with Harriet. It is very strange without the caravan. At the blacksmith, Dizzy watches as nails are hammered into Harriet's hooves.

"Does it hurt?" he asks her.

"Of course not!" says Harriet.

"Poor old Harriet!" says Dizzy every time the hammer hits a nail.

51

Harriet feels much better. She lets Bert ride on her back as she walks to the caravan. A little while later, Bert whispers to Dizzy, "I think we are going the wrong way."
Harriet is trotting quickly along the road.
"You must stop her," says Dizzy.

53

Bert pulls Harriet's mane and she stops.

"What is wrong?" asks Harriet.

"We are going the wrong way," says Dizzy. "We have lost the caravan."

They wander up lanes and over fields, but they they cannot find the caravan. Soon it begins to get dark. Suddenly, Harriet slips down a grassy bank. Bert flies over her head. There is a great, big SPLASH!

55

"Bert, where are you?" shouts Harriet. The moon comes out from behind a cloud and Harriet sees Bert. He is sitting in the middle of a pond, covered in weed.
"Where is Dizzy?" asks Bert.
Dizzy is sitting on Bert's head.
"Up here," shouts Dizzy, as he slides down into Bert's shirt.
"You are tickling me!" laughs Bert.

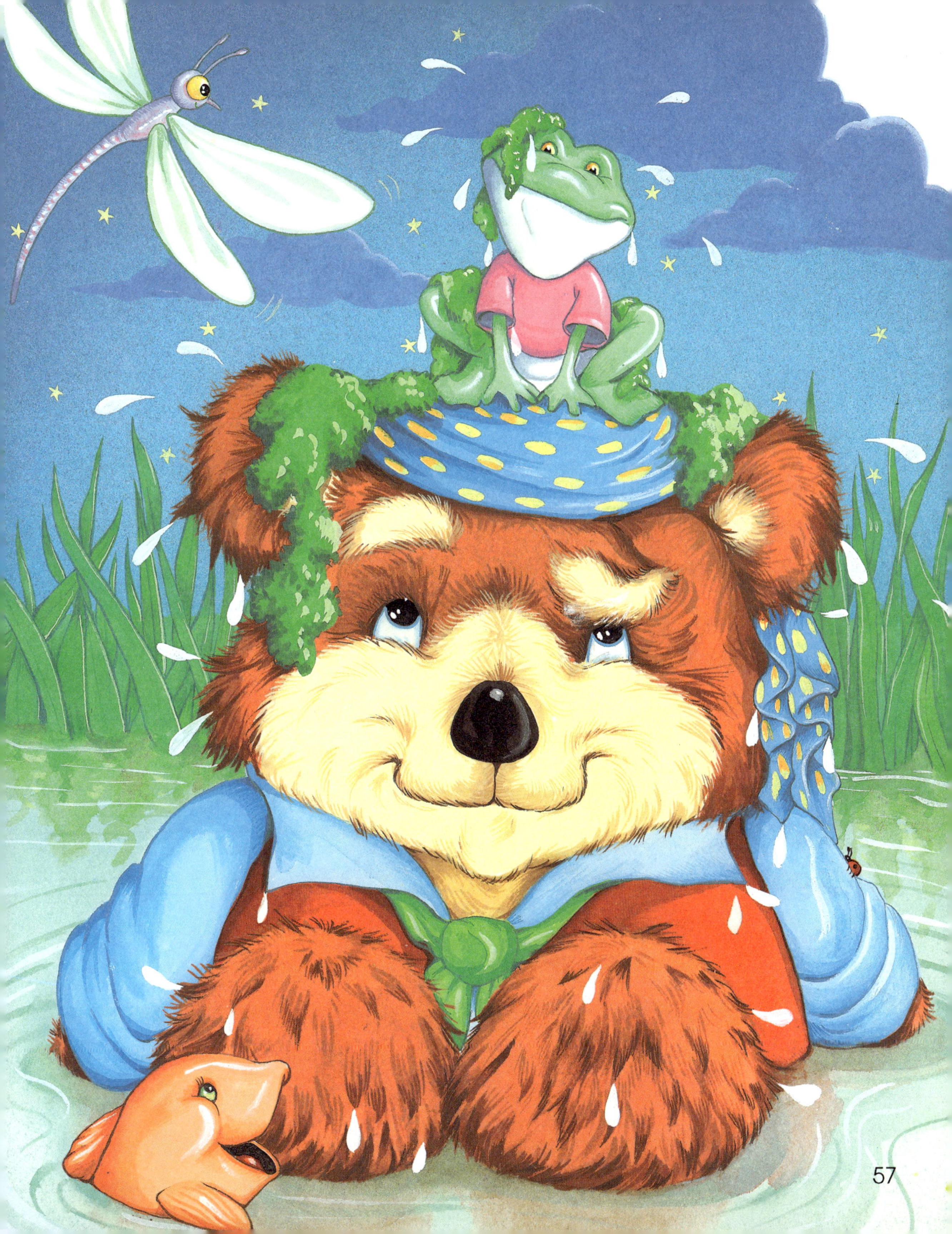

The more Dizzy moves, the more he tickles Bert, and the more Bert laughs.

"This is nothing to laugh about," says Harriet.

Bert manages to pull Dizzy out of his shirt. Dizzy is laughing, too. Even Harriet smiles. Bert pushes Harriet up the grassy slope. There, in front of them, is the caravan. "Of course, I knew it wasn't lost," says Harriet. Bert and Dizzy just smile.

59

Mud

It is a very windy day. Harriet is not happy. She does not like the way the road twists and turns.

"Why can't it be straight, like other roads?" she says. "I want to walk in a straight line."

Bert climbs down from the caravan and walks beside Harriet.

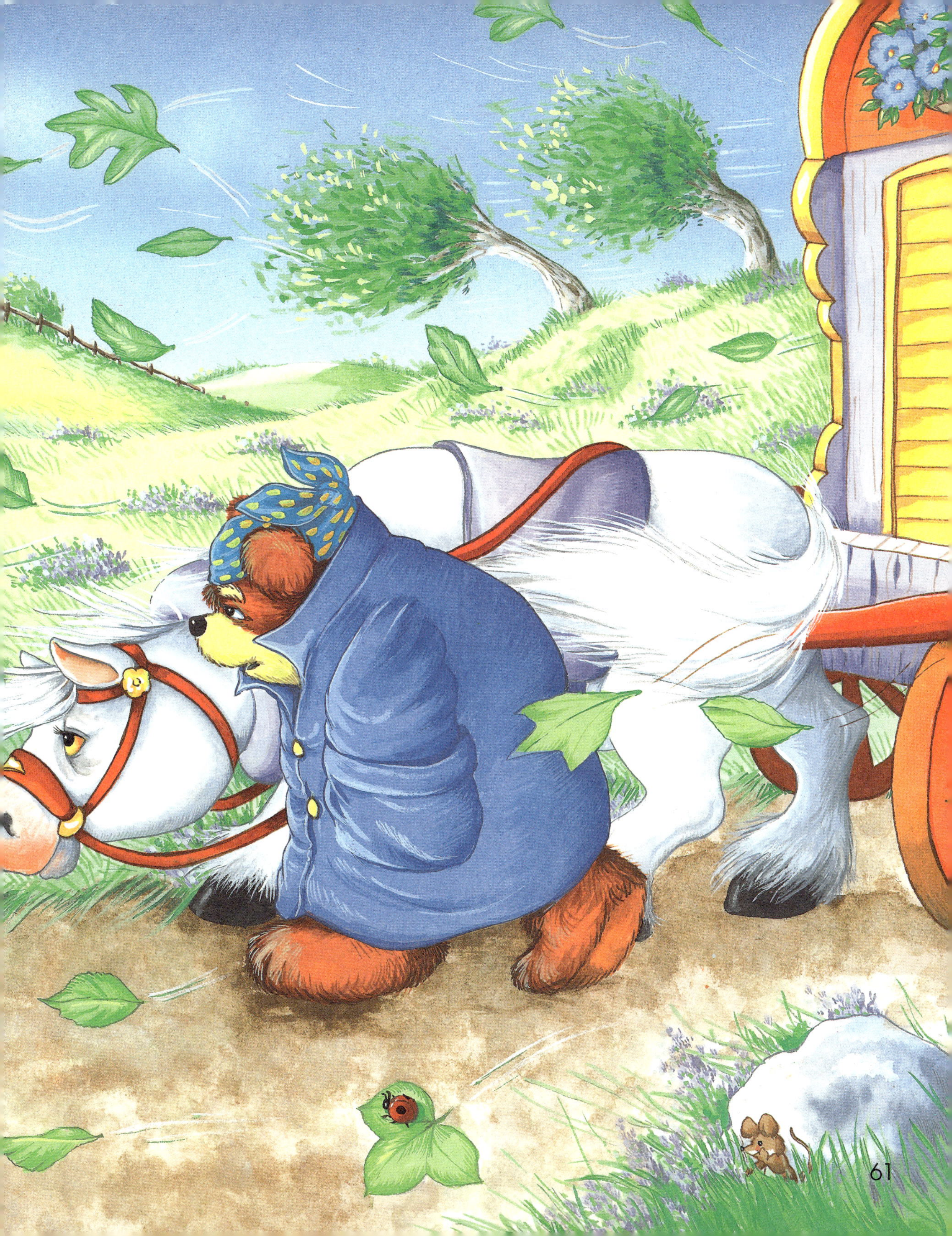

"I'll show them," says Harriet to herself. She steps off the road and onto the muddy grass, pulling the caravan with her. Dizzy's bucket makes a splish-splosh sound. "Harriet!" shouts Bert. "Stop it!" He tries to pull her back, but he isn't strong enough. "Stop it at once!"

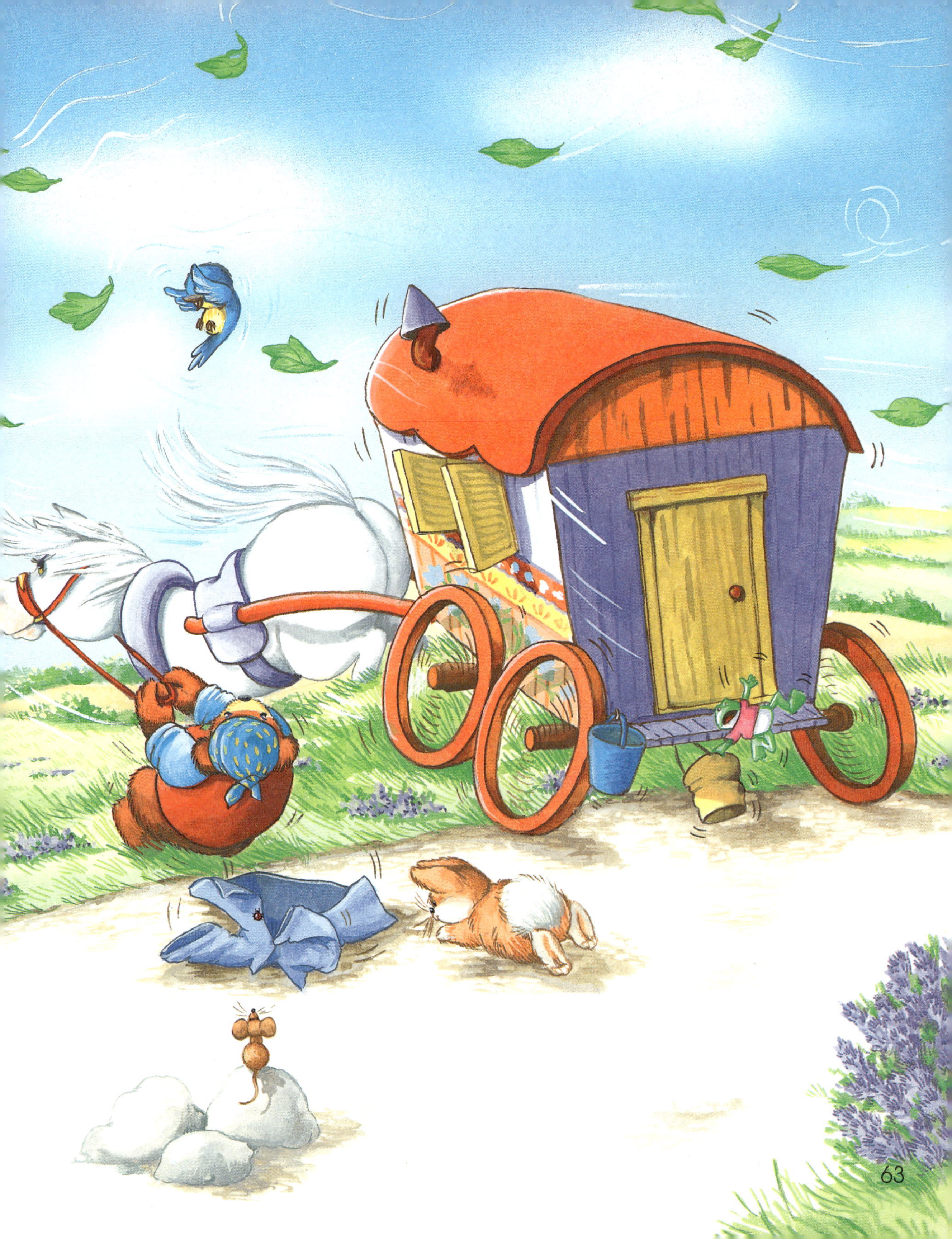

Suddenly Harriet does stop.
"Look at her feet!" says Dizzy. Bert looks to see Harriet's feet sinking in the mud.
"Help me, Bert," says Harriet.
As soon as Bert pulls one leg free, another one sinks into the mud.
"We must unhitch her from the caravan," says Dizzy.
"I'm frightened," says Harriet.

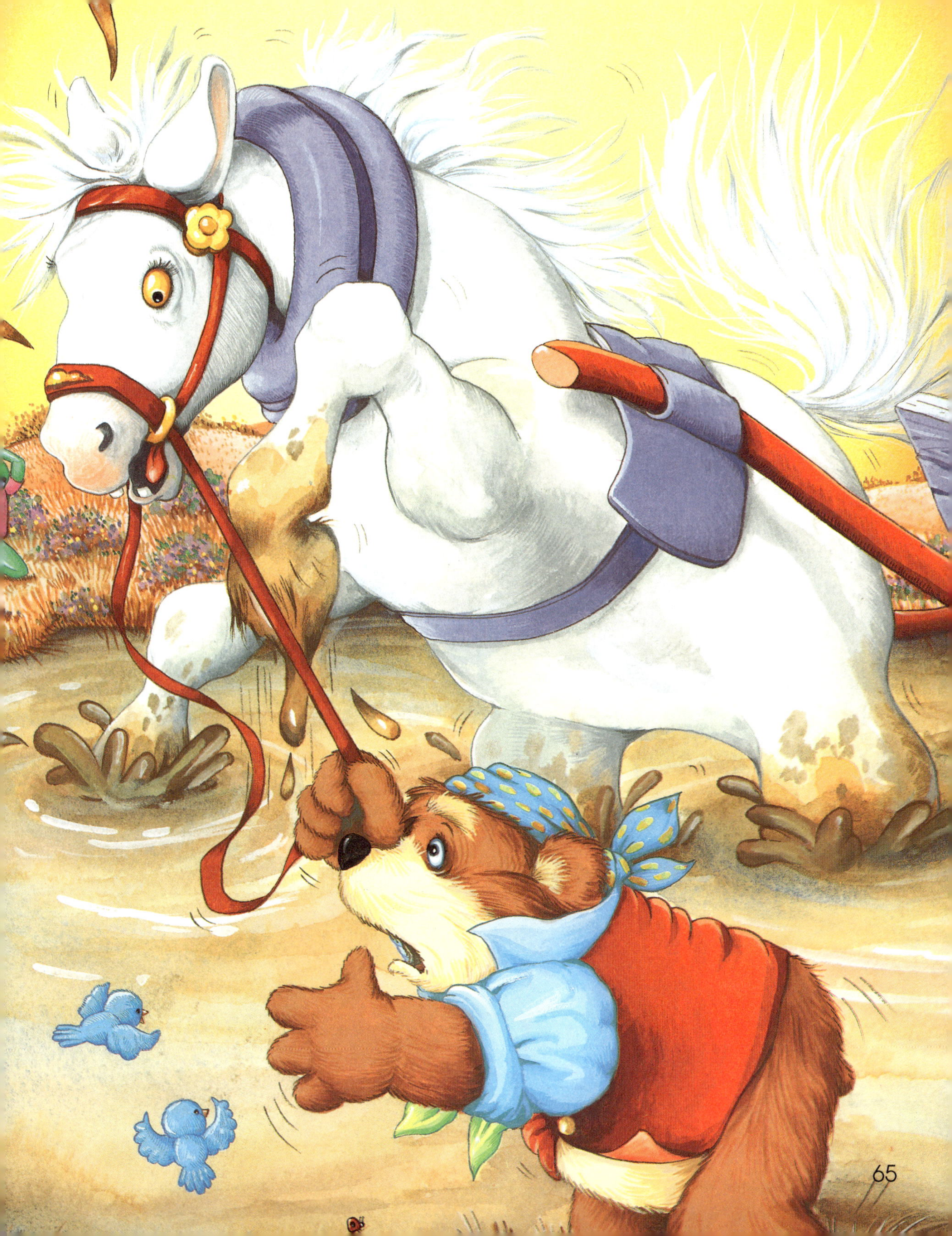

Bert unhitches Harriet from the caravan. She manages to pull herself out of the mud and back onto the road. Bert watches the caravan begin to sink. He is sad. "I'll fetch help," says Dizzy, and he hops away.

Bert reaches out for the rope at the back of the caravan. Harriet holds onto him so that he doesn't fall into the mud. At last Dizzy returns with a crowd of frogs.

67

The frogs are too light to sink into the mud. Bert cuts as much heather as he can from the roadside. The frogs pull it onto the mud and around the caravan. Soon there is a carpet of heather. The rope is tied to Harriet and she slowly drags the caravan over the heather and back to the road. "Three cheers for the frogs!" shouts Bert, throwing his hat in the air. "Hooray!" shouts Harriet, as loudly as she can.

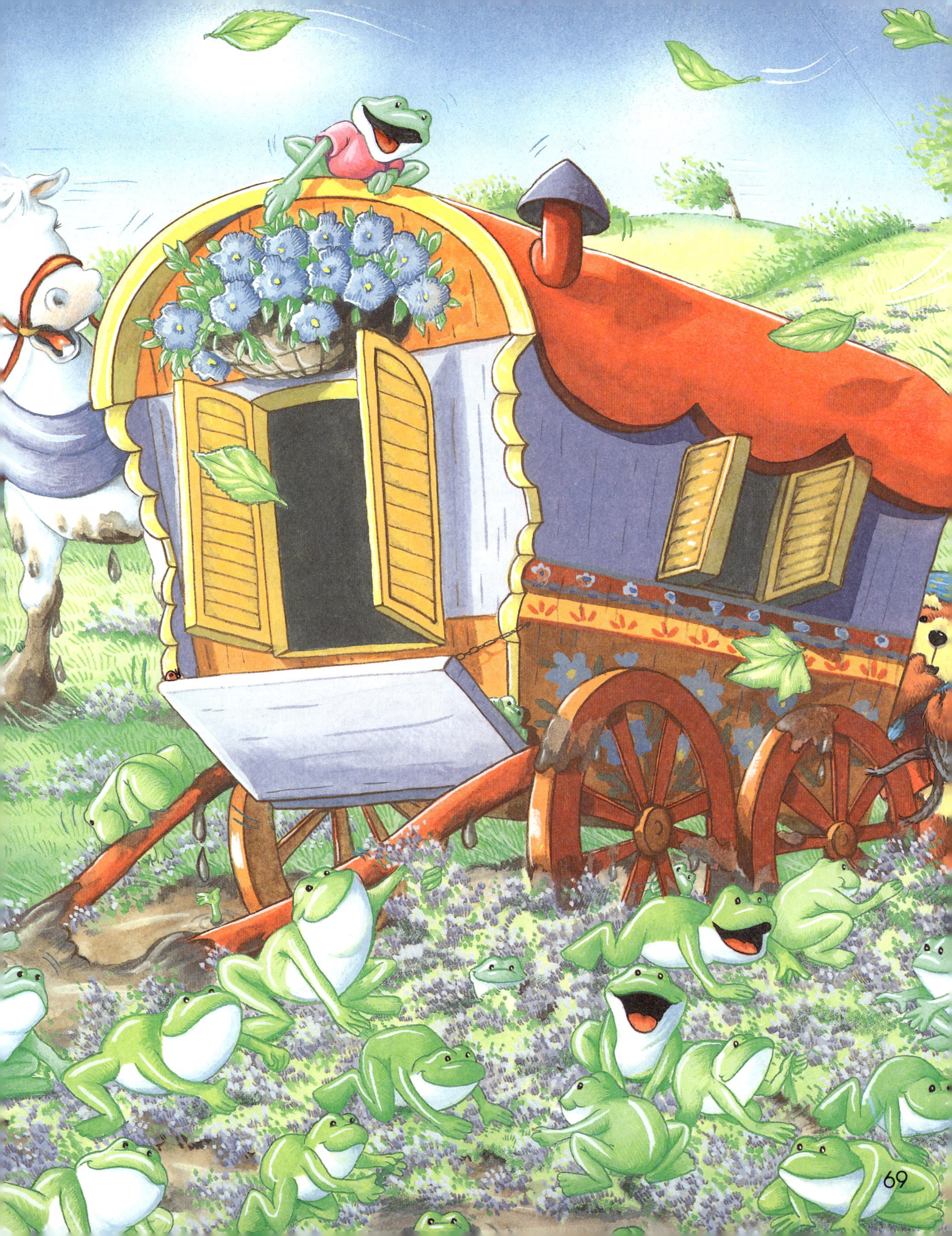

Atishoo!

Bert is lying in the sun. Harriet is busy eating grass. Dizzy is exploring. Suddenly Bert hears, "Atishoo!"
"Who's that?" asks Bert.
"It's me...aaatishoo!" says Dizzy.
"Are you getting a cold?" asks Bert.
"Frogs don't get colds! Atishoo! Atishoo!" says Dizzy.
"Try holding your breath," says Bert. Dizzy does this until his face is purple. Then he sneezes again.

71

"What is the matter with him?" asks Harriet.

"What do you think! Atishoo! Atishoo! Atishoo!" says Dizzy.

Bert picks Dizzy up and carries him into the caravan.

"Perhaps it's the sun," he says. He puts Dizzy on the table. Just as Dizzy thinks the sneezing has stopped - "Atishoo!" - he sneezes again.

73

The sneeze is so strong, that it throws Dizzy backwards into a bag of flour! Now Dizzy is covered in flour. He cannot see or hear. Bert cannot stop laughing.
"Help! Atishoo! Help! Help!" Dizzy jumps out of the caravan. He must find his bucket. Bert is still laughing.

75

"Atishoo!" says Dizzy. Where is his bucket? Bert tries to tell him, but he is laughing too much. Now Dizzy is bouncing towards Harriet. She looks down to see a white thing hopping around her legs. It hops under her tummy. She looks between her legs to see what it is. Suddenly the white thing bounces up and hits Harriet on the nose!

77

Harriet begins to jump and leap about. "Help me, Bert!" she shouts. But Bert is laughing even more. Poor Dizzy hops away as fast as he can. He still cannot see. Bert tries to grab hold of Harriet's tail to stop her jumping about. But he lies on the floor instead, laughing until tears fall down his face.

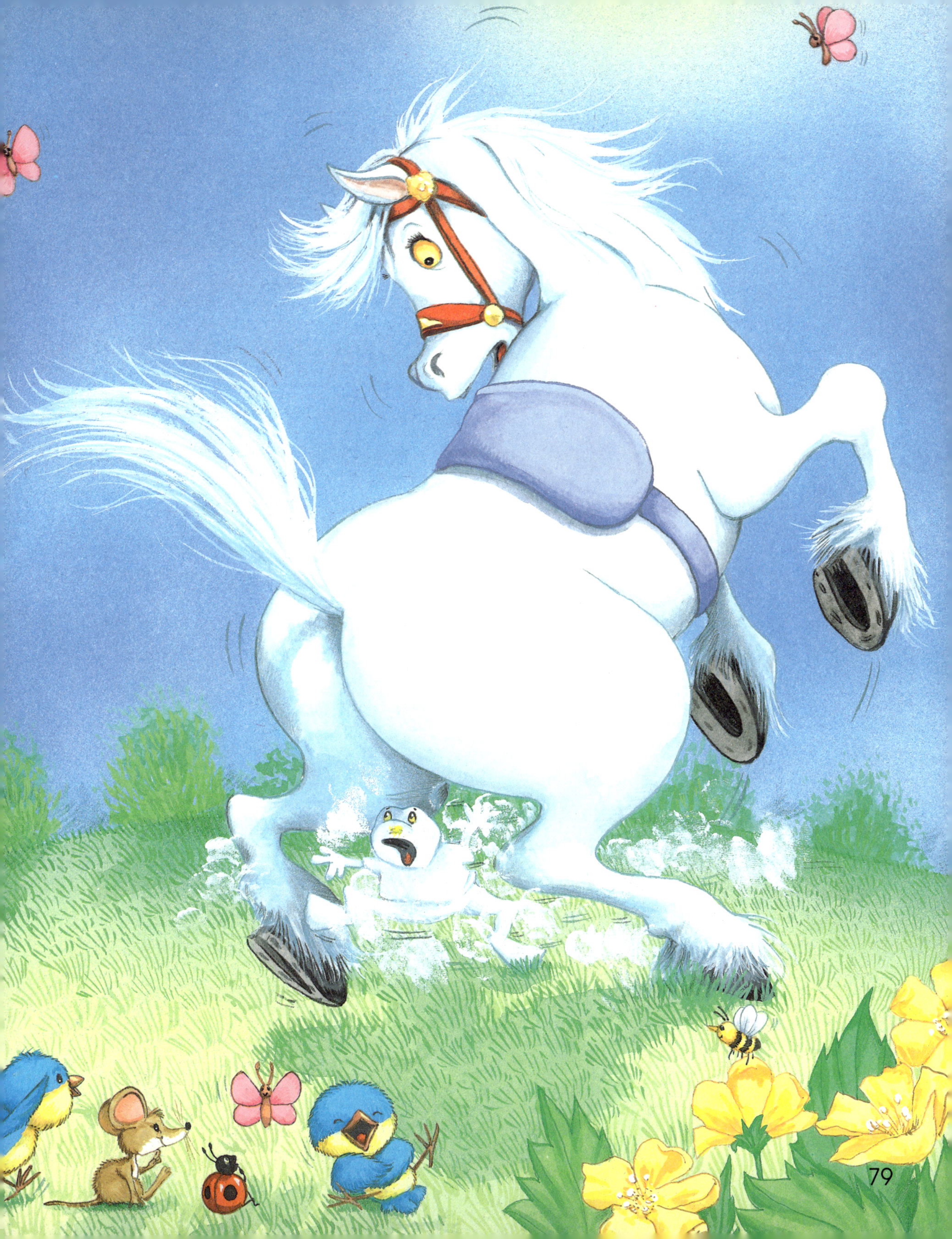

"Why is she jumping about?" says a voice in Bert's ear. It is Dizzy. He is still sneezing, but he has wiped the flour from his eyes and ears. Bert explains what has happened. Harriet gallops towards them and they both jump for safety - Dizzy under the fence and Bert over it.

81

Suddenly Harriet stops. "Why am I running around?" she asks Bert. Before Bert answers, Dizzy sneezes. "Why doesn't he wipe the pollen off his nose?" asks Harriet.
Bert looks at Dizzy's nose. It is yellow, like buttercup pollen. "Pollen always makes frogs sneeze," says Harriet.
"I didn't know that," says Bert. Neither does Harriet. She has made it up!

83

Bert finds a small paintbrush and cleans Dizzy's nose. It makes Dizzy laugh, but at least he isn't sneezing anymore.

"That will teach you not to put your nose into buttercups," says Harriet. "Now, why was I running about like that?"

Dizzy doesn't dare tell her. The less she knows about this adventure, the better!

85

Waves

"There is the sea," says Bert. They have stopped to give Harriet a rest. In the distance is the sea.
"Will we get any closer?" asks Harriet.
"We'll get right to the very edge," says Bert.
Dizzy is asleep in his bucket. Otherwise he would have a few questions to ask, too.

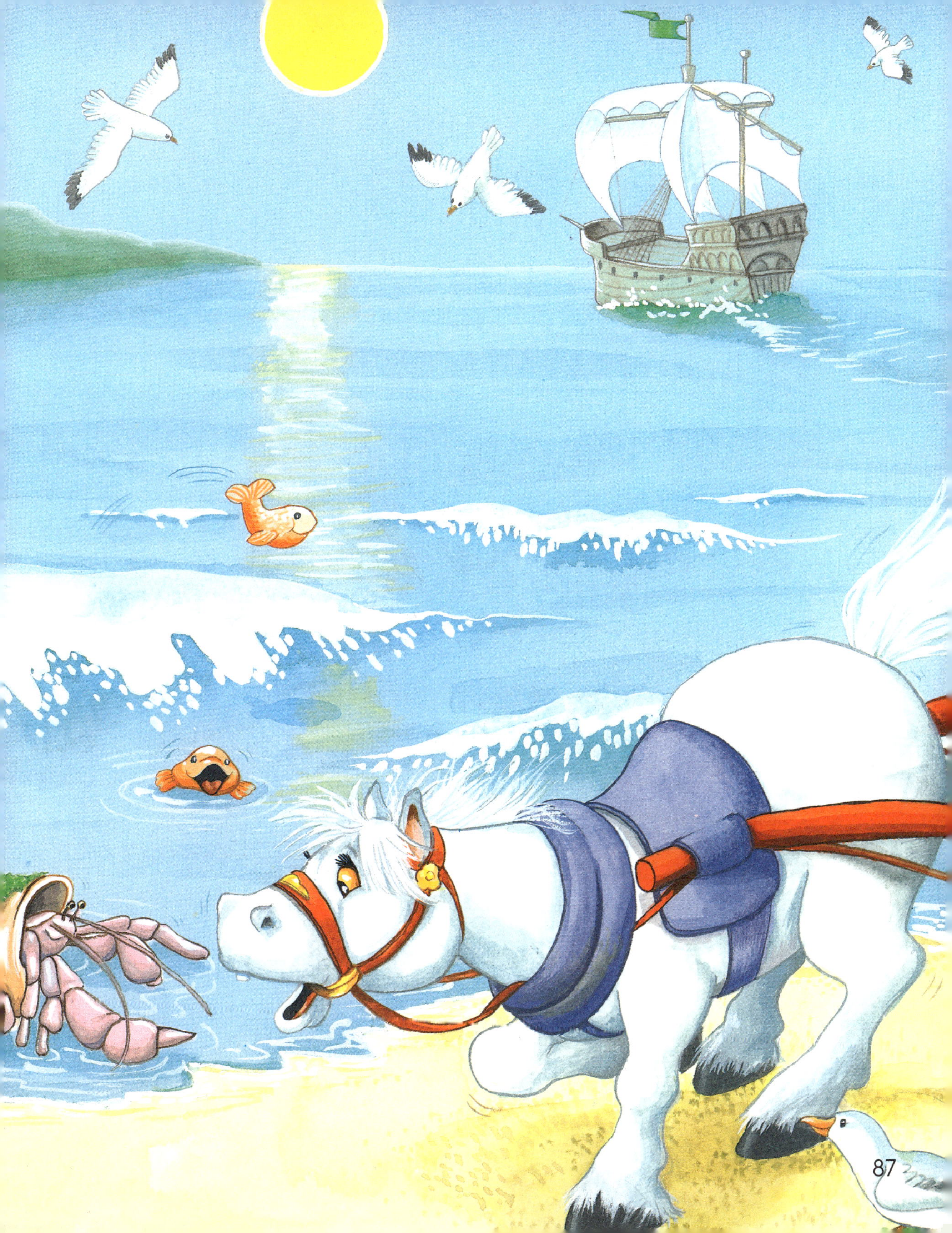

They are right beside the sea before Dizzy wakes up. He hops about with excitement. "What is all that water?" he asks.

"The sea, of course," says Bert in surprise. He thinks Dizzy knows what it is.

Suddenly Dizzy hops along the sand and dives into the water. As soon as he is in the sea, he is out again.

"Ugh! Why didn't someone tell me it is salty?" asks Dizzy.

89

Harriet wants to take a closer look at the sea. Bert unhitches her from the caravan. "You won't like it," warns Dizzy. "Come away!" Harriet does like the sea. She goes in a little deeper. She gallops backwards and forwards along the beach, through the waves. Bert sits and watches her. He has never seen her so happy. Dizzy sits beside him. Bert tells Dizzy stories of when he was young.

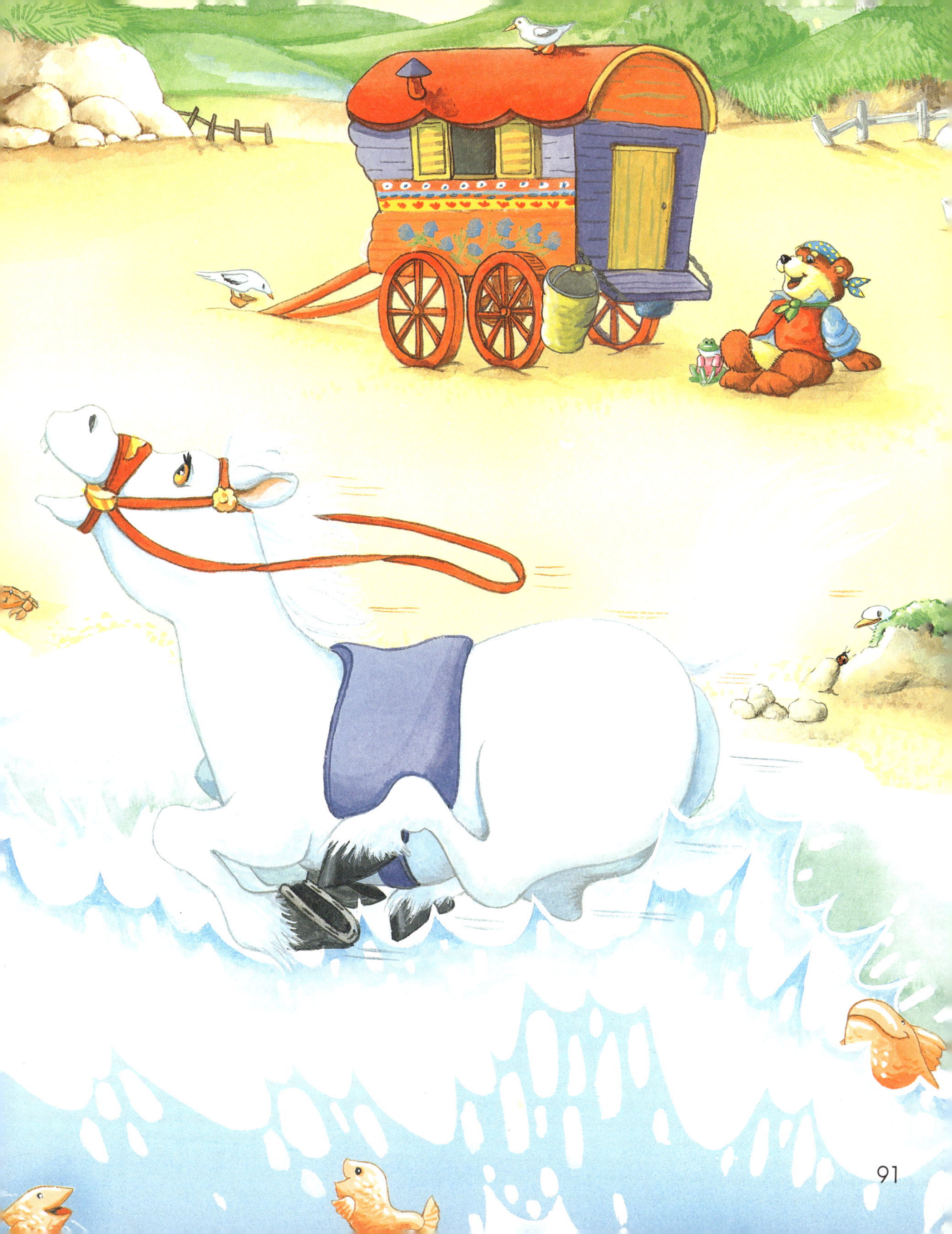

Soon the sun goes down. Harriet tells Bert she feels young again.
"I even understand why you like water so much, now," she says to Dizzy.
"Not the salty kind," says Dizzy.
"Oh, well," says Harriet. "Horses always have had more sense than frogs!" Then she plods off happily while Dizzy settles into his bucket of water that doesn't have a trace of salt in it.

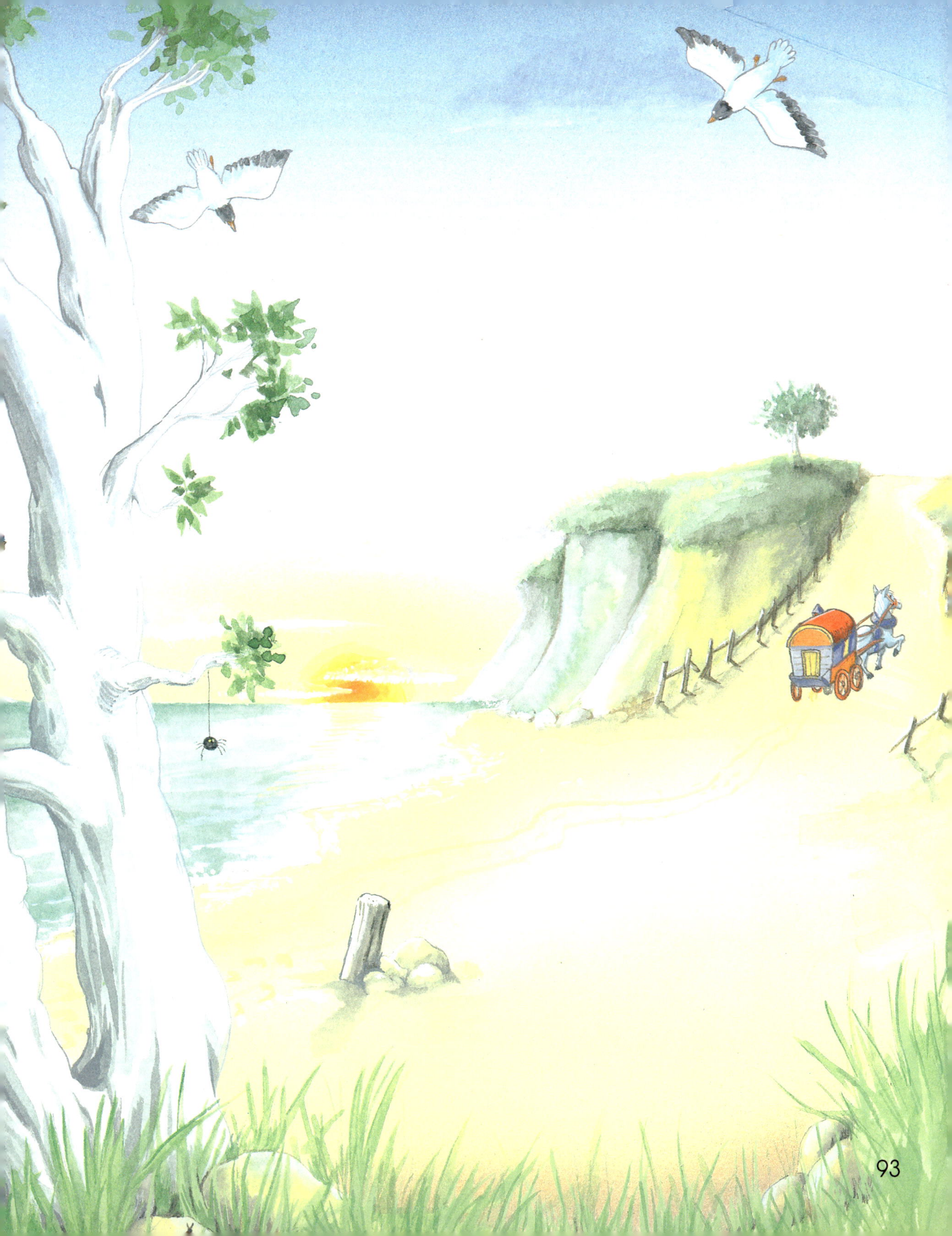

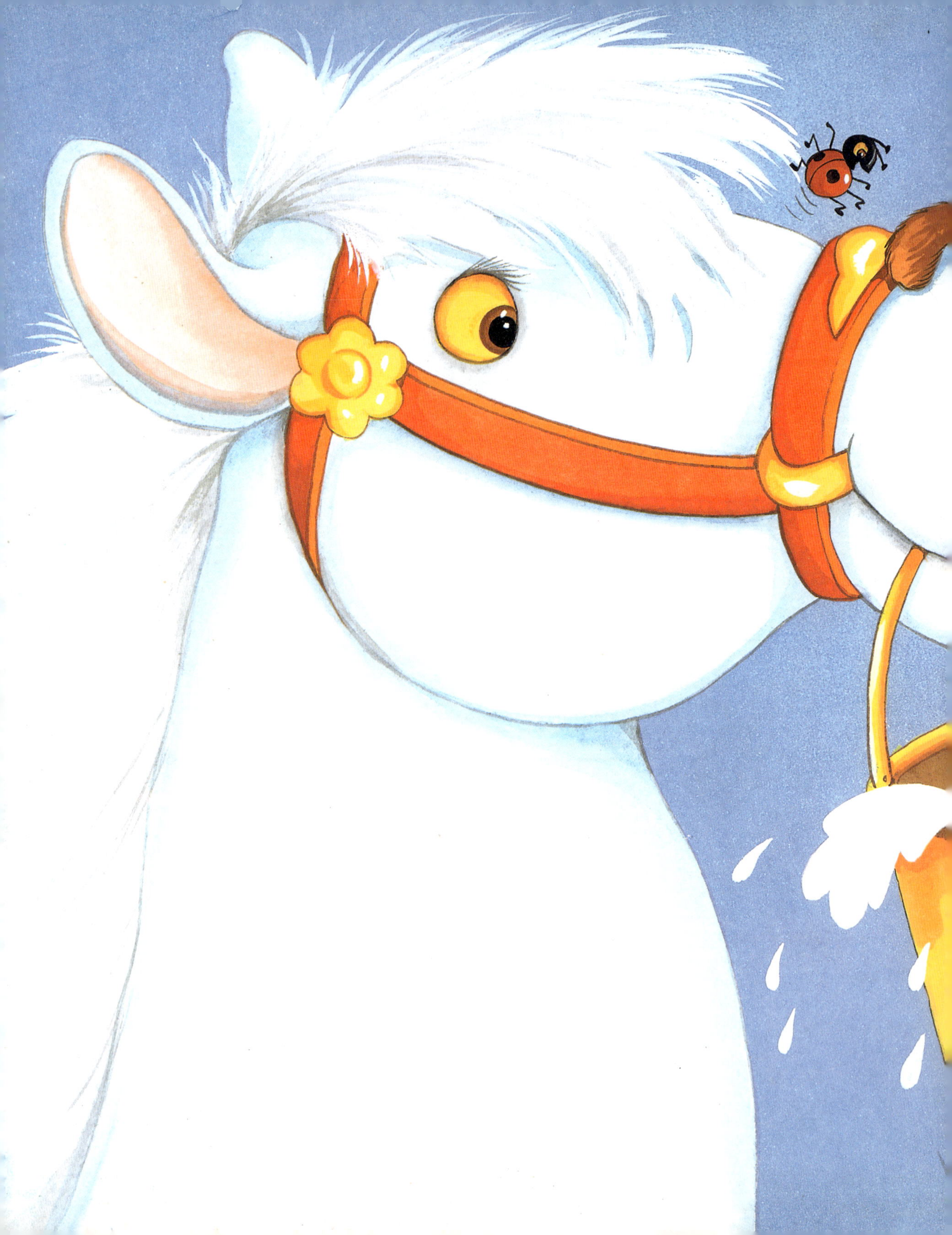